ROLLS-ROYCE

James Taylor

Published in Great Britain in 2017 by Bloomsbury Shire (part of Bloomsbury Publishing Plc), PO Box 883, Oxford, OX1 9PL, UK.

1385 Broadway, 5th Floor New York, NY 10018, USA.

E-mail: shireeditorial@ospreypublishing.com
www.shirebooks.co.uk

SHIRE is a trademark of Osprey Publishing, a division of Bloomsbury Publishing Plc.

A CIP catalogue record for this book is available from the British Library.

Shire Library no. 838.   ISBN-13: 978 1 78442 220 2

PDF e-book ISBN: 978 1 78442 222 6

ePub ISBN: 978 1 78442 221 9

XML ISBN: 978 1 78442 223 3

James Taylor has asserted his right under the Copyright, Designs and Patents Act, 1988, to be identified as the author of this book.

Typeset in Garamond Pro and Gill Sans.

Printed in China through World Print Ltd.

17 18 19 20 21   10 9 8 7 6 5 4 3 2 1

COVER IMAGE
Front cover: A 1911 Rolls-Royce Silver Ghost Barker Tourer on the Croatian coast (iStock).
Back cover: Hub cap from a Rolls-Royce Silver Spur (FieldsportsChannel TV/Flickr).

TITLE PAGE IMAGE
The Spirit of Ecstasy glides above a classic Rolls-Royce Grille. (Wikimedia Commons/Brian Snelson)

CONTENTS PAGE IMAGE
Rolls-Royce Phantoms were built in America as well as Britain and this one was bodied by Brewster for film star Tom Mix. The style was called the Playboy Roadster.

IMAGE ACKNOWLEDGEMENTS
BMW, pages 7, 10, 41; Bonhams 1793 Ltd/ Newspress, page 11; Coys Auctioneers/Newspress, pages 3, 44; Goodwood/Newspress, page 33 (bottom); H&H Classic Car Auctions/Newspress, pages 22 (bottom), 42 (top); Tony Hisgett/Wikimedia, page 13; Magic Car Pics, pages 14, 15 (both), 16 (top), 17, 18 (top), 19, 20, 21, 22 (both), 23, 24, 26, 27 (top), 29, 30, 32 (top), 34, 38, 39, 40, 41, 43 (top), 45, 46, 50, 51 (top), 53 (both); Mr Choppers/Wikimedia, page 27 (bottom); James Taylor Collection, page 43 (bottom); Newspress, pages 10 (top), 12, 16 (bottom); Rolls-Royce Motor Cars Ltd, pages 5 (both), 8, 9 (both), 28, 31, 32 (bottom), 33 (top), 42 (bottom), 47, 48, 49 (top), 51 (bottom), 52 (top), 54, 68 (bottom), 57 (both), 58 (both), 59 (both), 60 (both), 61 (both); Jagvar/Wikimedia, page 52 (bottom); Rolls-Royce Enthusiasts' Club, pages 4, 36 (both), 37; Silverstone Auctions Ltd, pages 49 (bottom), 56 (top); Terry Whalebone/Wikimedia, page 6.

Shire Publications is supporting the Woodland Trust, the UK's leading woodland conservation charity, by funding the dedication of trees.

CONTENTS

EARLY DAYS AND THE SILVER GHOST

IN THE EARLIEST days of motoring, cars were the playthings of the very rich, and were few and far between. They were noisy and unreliable, too, and a successful Manchester engineer called Frederick Henry Royce was deeply disappointed with the second-hand Decauville 10hp that he had bought in 1903.

Royce was able to buy the French-made car with money from the business he had set up as a young man of 21 in 1884. After training as a railway engineer, he had turned to making electrical items such as lampholders and bell sets, and later moved on to make dynamos and cranes. The business had expanded rapidly because of his insistence on quality and reliability.

He began tinkering with the Decauville, and by the end of March 1904 had designed a much-improved model

Henry Royce built three 10hp cars in 1904, and it was the excellence of their construction that attracted the interest of Charles Rolls. This was one of them, pictured at Cooke Street in Manchester in 1904.

FAR LEFT
Henry Royce
ran an electrical
business in
Manchester before
turning to cars.
This picture shows
him in later years;
he was created a
baronet in 1930
for his services to
British aviation.

LEFT
The Honourable
Charles Stewart
Rolls was in
business as an
importer of cars
when he was
introduced to
Royce. Impressed
by the quality
of Royce's 10hp
experimental cars,
he commissioned
a range of cars
from him, to
be marketed
as Rolls-Royce
models.

and built it with the aid of his staff. On 1 April 1904, the first Royce 10hp completed a journey of 15 miles without incident. Two similar prototypes followed, and one went to Henry Edmunds, a director of Royce Ltd. Edmunds was an experienced motorist and, realising how good the new car was, he mentioned it to his friend, the Honourable C.S. Rolls.

Charles Rolls was in business in London as CS Rolls Ltd with Claude Johnson, Secretary of the Royal Automobile Club, importing cars from the European continent. In May 1904 he travelled to Manchester to meet Royce and try the Royce 10hp for himself. There followed an agreement in December that CS Rolls Ltd would take all the cars Royce could build. There were two important stipulations. There was to be a range of four models – 10hp, 15hp, 20hp and 30hp types, as defined by the RAC at the time – and they should all be sold with the name of Rolls-Royce.

So Royce made arrangements for production, beginning with his existing 10hp design. He soon increased the size of its 1800cc twin-cylinder engine to 2000cc, and developed the larger models by scaling this up to provide the power that their bigger and heavier chassis needed. So the 15hp Rolls-Royce introduced in 1905 had a three-cylinder engine with 3000cc, the 20hp had four cylinders and 4000cc, and the 30hp had six cylinders and 6000cc. Although build quantities were small – the 20hp proved the most popular, with forty sold in two years – these chassis were very much appreciated by discerning buyers of the day. Clothed with bodywork to individual order by a coachbuilder of the customer's choice (Rolls-Royce never

This was the first 'production' model from Rolls-Royce, a 10hp twin-cylinder car built in 1905. This example belongs to the Science Museum and is usually displayed in the Manchester Museum of Science and Industry.

would provide its own bodies before 1946), they represented the pinnacle of motor car engineering in their time.

Royce's system of using common cylinder dimensions delivered the different sizes that CS Rolls Ltd wanted while avoiding production complications. However, Claude Johnson suggested that an ultra-silent town car to rival the electric town cars of the time might sell well. So in 1905, Royce produced a new engine with a 3500cc capacity and the V8 cylinder configuration then becoming popular in France for both car and aero engines. Three were built; just one was sold; but from this abortive experiment Royce learned lessons that were used on his later six-cylinder engines.

Sporting events provided car manufacturers with valuable publicity, and during 1906, Charles Rolls set about making the virtues of the Rolls-Royce motor car clear to the sport's followers. In May, he used a 20hp model to break the existing record for driving from London to Monte Carlo – despite an excessively long wait for a Channel ferry. In June, it was Claude Johnson whose 30hp was the only six-cylinder car to lose no points in the Scottish Reliability Trial. Then in September,

Rolls won the Isle of Man Tourist Trophy race in a 20hp. December saw the 20hp introduced to the USA, and Rolls promoted it by winning a race trophy with one in New York.

In the meantime, two more important events had taken place. First, in March 1906 a new company called Rolls-Royce Ltd had been established to make cars, buying out CS Rolls Ltd (although Royce's electrical company would remain active and separate until about 1933). Second, Royce had been working on an even better six-cylinder car model, and that had been introduced at the 1906 Olympia car show as the Rolls-Royce 40/50hp. The new seven-litre engine, with its cylinders cast in two blocks of three, was massively strong, with huge bearings and low mechanical stresses.

Available initially with both short and long chassis to take different types of bodywork, the 40/50 had simply outstanding silence and refinement in operation, and an example was prepared as a demonstrator. Claude Johnson had it painted an aluminium colour with silver-plated fittings and christened it the Silver Ghost to emphasise its silent running. This car ran with complete success in the 1907 Scottish Reliability Trials and immediately afterwards was driven between London and Glasgow 27 times – a formidable feat for a car of any kind in those days.

This magnificent 1909 40/50hp model has a Barker Roi des Belges body like that on the original Silver Ghost of 1907.

The famous Spirit of Ecstasy radiator mascot, also known as the Flying Lady, was commissioned in 1910. The artist was Charles Sykes; the model was Eleanor Thornton, long-time mistress of Baron Montagu of Beaulieu. In later years, some cars would carry a kneeling version of the mascot, to reduce height.

The reception accorded to the new 40/50 model was unprecedented. *Autocar* magazine called it the 'Best car in the world', an accolade that Rolls-Royce adopted as an advertising slogan. So during 1907, the company followed Claude Johnson's recommendation to end production of all its older models and focus entirely on building the 40/50 to the highest possible standards. Just over a hundred Rolls-Royce cars of other types had been made, but it was the 40/50 that really established the company's reputation worldwide. Today, the model is often referred to as the Silver Ghost, but in fact that name belonged only to the original factory demonstrator until 1925, when Rolls-Royce accepted it to distinguish the 40/50 from its replacement model.

Growing demand for Rolls-Royce chassis was by now putting pressure on space at the Manchester works. So the company found a new site at Derby and moved there in 1908. By this time, however, Charles Rolls was actively pursuing another of his interests; like many other wealthy young men of the time, he was fascinated by flying. He had actually suggested that Rolls-Royce should design an aero engine as early as 1907, but the company was too busy to move into another new field at the time. Rolls became a leading British pioneer of ballooning and flying, but in July 1910 was tragically killed when the tail broke off his Wright biplane during an aerial display at Bournemouth.

The strain of hard work was by now beginning to tell on Royce, and he was taken ill not long after Rolls' death. To lose the company's guiding light would have been a catastrophe at this stage, but Claude Johnson sagely arranged things so that Royce could work in peace and quiet, away from the pressures of the Derby factory. For the rest of his life, he would work from his house at West Wittering, on the south coast near Chichester, moving during the winter to the warmer climate of Le Canadel on the Mediterranean coast in south-east France.

In the meantime, the fashion for radiator mascots had led to some inappropriate ones being fitted to Rolls-Royce cars, so the

company commissioned a more suitable one in 1910. Royce himself thought the Spirit of Ecstasy (as it was called) hindered the driver's view, but it was fitted to most cars from 1911 and became standard in the early 1920s. It has been the company's most recognisable symbol ever since.

The 40/50 chassis remained in production until 1925, and a total of 6,173 were constructed at Manchester and Derby; exports went all over the world. Later chassis of course incorporated many changes, often to counter improvements on rival models. From 1909, a long-stroke 7428cc engine improved flexibility. In 1911, to counter publicity from rival chassis maker Napier, Rolls-Royce prepared a special car which ran all the way from London to Edinburgh on top gear, and subsequently added some of its special features to production cars.

This 1914 40/50 model typifies the appearance of a Rolls-Royce just before the Great War.

The six-cylinder side-valve engine of the 40/50 model was one of its outstanding features. It had two spark plugs for each cylinder to provide reliability, and a large centre main bearing to reduce vibration.

An electric starter was introduced – undreamt-of luxury for the day – and improvements to the brakes, cooling system and gearbox followed entries in the Austrian Alpine Trials between 1912 and 1914. As late as 1924 came four-wheel brakes with a mechanical servo. A mistake here cost the company dear: a premature announcement of the new brakes in October 1923 led to the company having to retro-fit them to large numbers of existing cars with the old two-wheel braking system.

Almost no two 40/50 cars were the same. Rolls-Royce provided only the chassis, and so customers turned to one of Britain's many coachbuilders for a hand-made body to suit their taste and requirements. Companies such as Barker and Hooper were among those who constructed coachwork to a huge variety of styles, aided by the long-bonnet proportions of the chassis. There were rakish skiffs, low-slung 'London to Edinburgh' type tourers, stately perpendicular limousines, coupés de ville and landaulettes, to list but a few.

Not surprisingly, the quality engineering and construction that went into a Rolls-Royce chassis made it expensive. Only the very wealthy could afford one, and their wealth allowed them to indulge their whims when ordering bodywork as well. Some of the most extravagant special Rolls-Royce cars

The vogue for Rolls-Royce motor cars among Indian royalty led to some extravagant creations such as this one, on a 40/50hp chassis dating from the early 1920s.

were created for Indian maharajas, as a craze for them swept the sub-continent's royalty. It had begun in 1908 when the Maharaja of Gwalior bought a special show car called the Pearl of India, and in later years some cars would carry extras such as searchlights to aid tiger-hunting parties in the dark.

One style of body that created its own legend was quite different. During the First World War, when the 40/50 chassis remained in limited production, 120 were bodied as armoured cars for use mainly in the Middle East. Periodically updated, these vehicles remained in use until 1941 – and some that were passed to the Irish Free State government lasted until 1944. Used by Col T.E. Lawrence for operations against the Turkish forces in 1917–18, these were the models that he described as 'more valuable than rubies' in *The Seven Pillars of Wisdom*.

In 1917, 40/50 production was suspended to allow Rolls-Royce to focus its efforts on the aero engines needed by the War Office, and which would go on to become another important business activity for the company. Chassis production for private buyers resumed in 1919, and demand was such that Rolls-Royce opened a second factory in 1921, this time at Springfield, Massachusetts, in the USA to cater

This is a later 40/50: a 1923 model built at the Springfield works in Massachusetts, USA. The salamanca body was built by New Haven for the Rolls-Royce Special Coachwork division. The early US-built cars had right-hand drive in the British style.

The high-quality leather upholstery, neatly fitted carpets and wooden capping rail on this 1911 40/50 defined motoring luxury at the time – and their descendants would continue to do so more than a century later.

for demand across the Atlantic. An initial batch of twenty-five chassis was constructed exactly to UK specifications, but later examples changed in minor respects to suit local conditions and some UK improvements (such as four-wheel brakes) never did cross the Atlantic. Just over 1,700 more 40/50 chassis were built at Springfield between 1921 and 1926.

Although many of the leading US coachbuilders worked on the 40/50 chassis, Rolls-Royce of America also had its own Rolls-Royce Custom Coachwork division, which provided a range of basic bodies. One notable coachbuilder was Brewster, which Rolls-Royce actually bought in 1925. Ernest Hives, later Rolls-Royce Chairman, once said, 'the best American bodies are better built and better finished than the English. They were made to more practical designs and have better fittings.'

However, by the early 1920s, the competition was becoming more intense. Chassis from the likes of Minerva, Hispano-Suiza, Isotta-Fraschini, Cadillac and Bentley were catching up fast – and in some cases offered features or qualities that the 40/50 did not have. So Royce developed new models to maintain his company's lead in the luxury car market.

TWENTIES AND PHANTOMS

THE MOTORING SCENE changed quite radically after the Great War ended. Sales of luxury models went into a decline, and at the same time the wealthy middle classes began to embrace car ownership. In recognition of this, Rolls-Royce embarked on a two-model policy, introducing a new and smaller model first alongside the existing and very grand 40/50.

This new model was called the Twenty and was a 20hp chassis aimed at the new breed of owner-driver. With a 3127cc engine that was under half the size of that in the 40/50, the car was also two feet shorter and weighed about half a ton less. It was an immediate success on its introduction in 1922, attracting a new breed of customer to the Rolls-Royce fold

The Twenty was often burdened with quite heavy coachwork, and this drove Rolls-Royce to develop the more powerful 20/25 model. This is a 1928 example, with the horizontal radiator shutters typical of the Twenty and a Park Ward landaulette body.

The bigger-bore engine in the 20/25 was an overhead-valve six-cylinder of 3669cc. It had a cast-iron cylinder block and head on an aluminium crankcase and delivered the power needed for the heavy bodies that customers so often specified.

but maintaining the marque's reputation for extremely high standards of reliability and refinement.

Many owners came from the professional classes – doctors, lawyers and the like – and they tended to avoid flamboyant bodywork in favour of more discreet and conventional styles. Many of these bodies were heavy by their very nature, and so the 'small' Rolls-Royce earned a reputation for being rather slow. The change to a four-speed gearbox in 1925 helped acceleration a little, and four-wheel brakes arrived at the same time. Horizontal radiator shutters were a distinguishing feature of those built up to 1928. Just 2,940 of these cars were built before they were replaced in 1929, by which time they looked almost embarrassingly slow against cheaper alternatives.

So the engine was bored out to give more power, and the Twenty gave way in 1929 to the 20/25 model. This one went down very well, and sold more than twice as strongly as the contemporary 'big' Rolls-Royce, the Phantom I; a total of 3,827 were sold to make this the most popular Rolls-Royce model of the inter-war years. It was noted for exceptional flexibility on the top gear of its four-speed gearbox, for better brakes than its predecessor (thanks to an improved servo), and for its remarkably silent running. Late examples were capable of as much as 75mph, depending of course on the type of body fitted.

There were some delightful bodies on the 20/25 chassis, by coachbuilders such as HJ Mulliner and Freestone & Webb,

The 'small' Rolls-Royce also attracted lighter and more sporting bodywork, of course, like the Special Touring Saloon body by Park Ward on this 1934 example.

Gurney Nutting created some of the most attractive bodies on Rolls-Royce chassis in the 1930s, and this sedanca de ville style was available on both the 20/25 and the Phantom chassis, as well as on other makes.

who were at the height of their powers in the early 1930s. Hooper built some attractive close-coupled saloons, and Gurney Nutting some sublime sedanca coupés. But this was also a time when the coachbuilding industry was flirting with streamlining, which sometimes compromised the lines for the sake of fashion. Many buyers of the 20/25 also turned for their bodywork to smaller and less skilled coachbuilders, whose products may have been more affordable but sometimes let down the quality of the chassis.

Highly regarded coachbuilder Thrupp & Maberley was responsible for the drophead coupé body on this 1934 20/25 chassis.

In the meantime, Royce had developed a replacement for the ageing 40/50 model. The new 'large' Rolls-Royce was introduced in 1925 with the name of Phantom, and in the early days was often described as the New Phantom. In practice, it turned out to be something of an interim design, because chassis, suspension, gearbox and brakes were more or less unchanged from the 40/50. What was new was the engine, now with modern overhead valves in place of the 40/50's side valves, and with a longer stroke and narrower

Some customers had their chassis bodied by the best continental European coachbuilders, and this attractive cabriolet was by the Swiss master Graber, on a 1932 20/25.

bore to reduce road tax liability under the RAC rating system that then obtained in Britain. Its capacity of 7668cc was also slightly greater than that of the 40/50.

The Phantom's extra power was very welcome, but the downside was that the new chassis was much heavier than the old – by around 600lb. It still stood high off the ground on the cantilever springs of the 40/50, it had a taller radiator, and it entered production at a time when very large free-standing headlights were in vogue. All this did nothing for wind resistance, and Phantoms could rarely exceed 75–80mph, especially when fitted with the square-rigged formal bodywork that so many owners ordered. And many bodies were indeed rather dull, even though there were also some exotic creations for Indian princes in this period.

Phantoms were built at Springfield, too, adding 1,240 chassis to the 2,212 built at Derby. As some modifications were needed to create left-hand drive versions, their production did not begin until 1926, and the American chassis came with the benefit of a one-shot Bijur chassis lubrication system that Derby Phantoms did not have. By contrast with the British

The 'large' Rolls-Royce was the Phantom from 1925, and this example bears the sporting drophead coupé bodywork that went so well with the chassis.

Now with nearly 7.7 litres, the six-cylinder engine of the Phantom boasted a modern overhead valve design, although the chassis was little changed from that of the 40/50.

The short-coupled saloon body on this 1929 Phantom II chassis was built by Weymann, and has the fashionable faux-cabriolet look.

cars, the Springfield Phantoms often had very handsome coachwork, and some of the phaetons and town cars built by Brewster (still using their own name) were exceptional. Springfield chassis assembly ended in 1931, two years after that at Derby, although some chassis seem to have been built as late as 1933.

Well aware of the Phantom's performance shortcomings, Royce took care to redesign the large Rolls-Royce chassis

comprehensively in the mid-1920s. In particular, he changed the suspension so that the cars sat lower to the ground – they were as much as 9 inches lower when formal closed bodies were fitted. The Phantom II was introduced in 1929 and was a very modern design that now incorporated the one-shot central lubrication system and could be had with short or long wheelbases. Although the engine was the same size as that of the older Phantom, it now boasted modern overhead valves and an efficient cross-flow cylinder head for greater power and performance. The gearbox, too, was now attached to the engine for the first time rather than mounted separately.

The new low-slung chassis combined with the long bonnet gave the coachbuilders an ideal basis for their creations. The best of them delivered some beautiful coupés, sedancas and drophead coupés, but perhaps the most elegant were seen on the special Continental chassis that accounted for about 17 per cent of those built. This had taller gearing that allowed for more relaxed high-speed cruising, and was designed for exactly that on the long clear roads of the European continent. A maximum of more than 90mph was possible on late models, by which time engine power had

This athletic-looking short-chassis Phantom II Continental has a drophead coupé body by Freestone & Webb and dates from 1932. The car has a dickey seat, a rare feature on the Continentals.

The Phantom II was also a natural choice for those who wanted a grand chauffeur-driven vehicle, and this is a sedanca de ville body by Park Ward on a 1930 chassis. It was delivered to an American lady when new.

been increased and the gearbox had been given synchromesh on all but bottom gear.

Sadly, the Phantom II was the last car that Royce himself would design. In 1933, he fell ill and died at West Wittering; he was seventy years old. Shortly afterwards, the double-R emblem on Rolls-Royce radiator grilles changed from red to black, and understandably this was long assumed to be a mark of respect or mourning. The reality, however, was more prosaic: the company had planned the change for some time, as the red had clashed with some of the more extravagant colours that customers were ordering in increasing numbers.

Meanwhile, Rolls-Royce had been able to remove one of its competitors from the market, when it bought the ailing Bentley company in 1931. Bentley was a maker of high-quality chassis with a more sporting nature than those of Rolls-Royce, and the Phantom II Continental had been a nod in their direction. Most worrying to Rolls-Royce was the magnificent 8-litre model introduced in 1930, although the 4-litre derived from it in a hurry to compete with the 20/25 as financial trouble began to bite was less of a problem. Both these cars were removed from the market in 1931 (although a few lingered on unsold), but Rolls-Royce would use the Bentley name on a new and very successful range of sporting chassis from 1933.

Rolls-Royce, too, suffered from the effects of the Depression, and one result was that only 1,680 Phantom II chassis were sold before the model was replaced in 1935. Replaced it had to be, too, because developments by rival makers were making it uncompetitive. The early 1930s brought a rash of V12 engines from makers such as Packard in America and Hispano-Suiza in Europe, and even a V16 from Cadillac. As even medium-priced American cars began to appear with independent front suspension, the ride quality of the Phantom II lost its superiority.

So when the replacement Phantom III was designed, it had a magnificent and complicated 7.3-litre V12 engine and a Rolls-Royce modified independent front suspension licensed from General Motors in the USA. The chassis was rigidly braced to allow the suspension to work at its best, the top three speeds in the gearbox had synchromesh, and there was a further improved central chassis lubrication system.

HJ Mulliner built the elegant sedanca de ville body on this 1937 Phantom III. The chassis had its radiator over the front axle rather than behind, as on earlier Phantoms, giving a characteristic long-bonnet look.

This was the magnificent V12 engine in the Phantom III. As always, the presentation mattered just as much as the performance and reliability.

Power was increased by 12 per cent over the Phantom II's six-cylinder engine, and then again by a further 10 per cent later in production.

A car this ambitious and complicated, and built to Rolls-Royce standards, was inevitably also formidably expensive. Its cost had two main results: first, many would-be

Luxury in the rear seat of a Phantom III – which was where most owners sat. Note the contemporary fashion for a pleated backrest combined with plain cushions.

owners shied away and chose the smaller Rolls-Royce instead; and second, very few owners bought such a chassis to have it fitted with frivolous or lightweight sporting bodywork. Most Phantom IIIs had deliberately grand (and therefore heavy) bodies, not all of them wholly successful. Changed front-end proportions, with the radiator now firmly ahead of the front wheels rather than above the axle centre-line, provided new challenges for the body designers. Just 727 of these superb machines were built before the outbreak of war in 1939 brought production to an end (although assembly in fact continued until orders had been fulfilled).

The small Rolls-Royce was also updated in the middle of the decade, as the 20/25 model gave way to the more powerful 20/30. This car shared its new 4¼-litre engine with the sporting Bentley, although its chassis was essentially a longer-wheelbase version of that on the 20/25. Maximum speed and acceleration both benefited on cars with appropriately light bodywork, but a consequence of the Phantom III's high cost was that many buyers had the heavy, formal coachwork they wanted built onto a 20/30 chassis instead. Yet there were some undeniably attractive creations on many of the 1,201 chassis built between 1936 and 1938.

The 25/30 chassis brought a larger engine, and this 1938 example was bodied as an elegant sports saloon by Hooper, which had held a Royal Warrant since 1830. The two-tone claret and black is very subtle, and cleverly lightens the car's appearance.

WAR AND TRANSITION

THE LATER 1930S saw Rolls-Royce buyers turning increasingly to the smaller models, choosing a 25/30 in preference to the large, expensive and complex Phantom III. So when work began on developing the 25/30's replacement, the company planned an extra 4 inches of wheelbase that would give enough length for formal and chauffeur-driven bodywork.

To improve the ride, they added a version of the independent front suspension used on the Phantom III, and to make the most of this they braced the chassis in much the same way as on the larger car. For the first time, the chassis members were also welded rather than riveted together. There was also a variable ride control feature, which stiffened or softened the action of the dampers from a lever on the steering wheel and added further refinement to the ride. Built-in hydraulic jacks to aid wheel changing were another innovation.

For extra performance, what was more or less the Bentley version of the 4¼-litre engine with its efficient cross-flow cylinder head was added into the mix, while the gearbox came with synchromesh on its top three gears. On its introduction in October 1938, the new Rolls-Royce Wraith was capable of more than 80mph with very high levels of refinement, but there were faster and cheaper chassis available from Daimler and Lagonda with almost as much refinement.

The Wraith had a short production run due to the outbreak of war in 1939; just 491 chassis had been built before production was halted to allow Rolls-Royce to concentrate on aero engines. Many chassis were given the rather staid and heavy saloon or limousine bodies that the company had anticipated, although there were a few attractive exceptions with lighter coachwork.

The familiar Rolls-Royce ingredients were present inside the Hooper saloon on Silver Dawn chassis. The upholstery on this one was pleated, reflecting changing fashions.

Though considerably smaller than the Phantom, the 1938 Rolls-Royce Wraith was still a large car. This limousine-bodied example appears to have been used at one stage by a funeral parlour: note the roof rack for carrying floral tributes.

While the Wraith was being developed, changes were under way at the Derby works. By the mid-1930s, Rolls-Royce was finding its car sales were slowing down and were no longer profitable. Although the aero engines were keeping the company solvent, they were also taking engineering design time away from the cars. So as a first step, the company was divided into separately managed Aero and Car Divisions during 1937.

It was also quite clear that the three car chassis being produced at the time had too little in common with one another, and the Rolls-Royce 25/30, Phantom III and Bentley 4¼-litre all had different technical problems that placed demands on the engineers' time. Out of this realisation was born an ambitious plan to develop a 'rationalised' range of products. Rolls-Royce and Bentley chassis would share as many common components as possible; wheelbase lengths would be shared among models; and there would be four-cylinder, six-cylinder and eight-cylinder derivatives of a common engine design. There would even be some common body designs, no doubt from Park Ward, the coachbuilder that Rolls-Royce would buy in 1939. A mix-and-match policy would allow a healthy variety of different models.

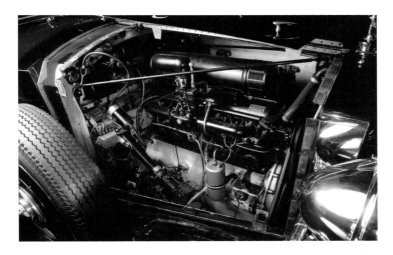

The Wraith's engine was essentially the same as the one used in the contemporary Bentley, a 4¼-litre six-cylinder with overhead valves.

It was a plan that would go through many iterations before taking its final shape, and a projected third range of smaller models never came to production, but it underpinned the entire Rolls-Royce and Bentley product range that appeared after the war ended in 1945. During that war, the Derby factories had been turned over completely to aero engine production, and the British government also asked Rolls-Royce to manage a 'shadow factory' at Crewe, where its production was duplicated both to gain additional volumes and to reduce the risk of a bombing raid disrupting production completely.

The Wraith was always a coachbuilt car, and some gained very interesting coachwork. This 1938 car was bodied for French actress Gaby Morlay as a coupé by the highly individual coachbuilder De Villars.

There were several broadly similar touring saloon designs for the post-war Silver Wraith, and this is one by Hooper. Spats and half-spats for the rear wheels were in fashion around 1950. Note the under-chassis radio aerial on this car.

As the new strategy for car production involved increased volumes and other alterations, the Car Division moved to the larger Crewe factory when the war ended, and resumed operations there from 1946.

Rolls-Royce set out its stall very deliberately in 1946 with two new models. First impressions suggested a return to the pre-war range of a large model and a smaller one, but it was not quite that simple. The company knew that its survival would depend on the production rationalisation planned before the war, and the two new models were closely related. One was not even a Rolls-Royce but a Bentley, called the Mk VI; the Rolls-Royce name was reserved for the large car, which was called the Silver Wraith.

Both cars had variants of the same basic engine, which had the same bore and stroke dimensions as the pre-war 4¼-litre type but had been completely redesigned with a new one-piece cylinder block and a new cylinder head with larger valves in an inlet-over-exhaust configuration. But the major shock for buyers was that the smaller car now came with a 'standard steel' body, built to a standardised design by Pressed Steel. It was undeniably attractive, picking up and modernising elements of the razor-edge design that had been popular in the late 1930s, but it removed the buyer from the process of ordering bespoke coachwork.

Rolls-Royce suspected that its clientele might not take readily to the new arrangements, and this was one reason why it had made the standardised car available only as a Bentley. The larger Rolls-Royce was, by contrast, sold in the traditional way as a chassis for which the buyer could order a bespoke body; and, playing for safety, the company made the new Bentley chassis available for custom coachwork as well. However, only around one in five buyers took up that option. Times had changed.

One factor was that the numbers of coachbuilders, both in Britain and on the European continent, had drastically declined. Among the reasons for this was that many car makers were turning to monocoque structures in which there was no separate chassis, and therefore no opportunity for the coachbuilder to perform his traditional work. Those coachbuilders that had survived the war also had to think in terms of production economies, and as a result increasingly favoured batch construction of designs that could be altered in minor respects to suit individual requests. So there was a very much reduced variety among bodies on the new post-war models.

Again bodied by Hooper, this time as a limousine with division, this is the long-wheelbase Silver Wraith chassis. The car dates from 1953.

The first post-war Rolls-Royce, then, was the Silver Wraith. Its name deliberately suggested a link to the pre-war Wraith and its chassis followed much the same pattern, but was in fact completely new. The independent front suspension now had anti-dive geometry, and overall the chassis was very nearly as refined as its predecessor while being rather less costly to manufacture. More performance was added in 1951 with an increase in engine size to 4566cc, and then again in 1955 when it went up to 4887cc. A long-wheelbase chassis became optional in 1951, and from 1953 buyers could order a US-made General Motors Hydramatic automatic gearbox – modified, of course, by Rolls-Royce. The automatic gearbox became standard in 1955, and power-assisted steering became an option a year later.

Though it was a descendant of the smaller Rolls-Royce models of the 1930s, the Silver Wraith was treated very much as the senior model of the range. The majority of bodies ordered for it were saloons and limousines; coupé and drophead coupé designs were comparatively rare. Many early bodies picked up the razor-edge fashion, just as the Bentley Mk VI had done, but tastes were changing and coachbuilders sometimes struggled to accommodate the newer ideas.

The new two-model strategy generally worked well, but Rolls-Royce had not allowed for the fact that the Bentley name was little known in the USA, making buyers there wary of the smaller car. The solution came in 1949 with a Rolls-Royce

The long-wheelbase Silver Wraith incorporated folding occasional seats in the rear, behind the division. The interior, with the plain leather panels fashionable at the time, is as luxurious as ever.

version of the Mk VI planned initially only for export. Slightly less powerful than the Bentley, to help preserve that car's more sporting character, the new Rolls-Royce Silver Dawn shared its standard steel bodywork but had a different dashboard and – to suit American tastes – a column gearchange.

Like the Silver Wraith, the Silver Dawn took on the more powerful 4566cc engine in 1951, and then the option of an automatic gearbox in 1952, when the body was also modified with the larger boot introduced on the Bentley (newly renamed an R-type) at the same time. In October 1953, the smaller Rolls-Royce finally became available in Britain as well, although by this stage it had only two years of production left.

One result of these complicated arrangements was that the Silver Dawn remained quite rare, only 760 being built in six years of production; the Bentley equivalent was far better known in most countries, and especially in Britain. By far the majority of Silver Dawn chassis had standard steel bodywork, but a few were ordered with coachbuilt bodies, most notably a drophead coupé design by Park Ward.

Yet the combination of Silver Dawn and Silver Wraith was not quite enough to satisfy demand for Rolls-Royce chassis in the early 1950s. There was a demand, albeit limited, for large and formal chassis to suit limousine and parade cars for heads

The Silver Dawn was really the Rolls-Royce version of the Bentley Mk VI, with a less powerful engine. This is the later 'big boot' version, and is an export model with left-hand drive.

The Silver Dawn was also available as a chassis for coachbuilt bodywork. Hooper built this example in 1954; Freestone & Webb offered a similar and arguably even more attractive design.

of state and royalty, and to satisfy this, the company fell back on its rationalised range strategy.

Such a chassis, larger than the Silver Wraith that otherwise topped the range, could only be called a Phantom, and the Phantom IV it duly became. Its chassis followed the design principles of the existing production models, but was longer and had additional bracing to maintain rigidity. Its engine was an eight-cylinder version of the six-cylinder type seen in the Silver Wraith and Silver Dawn, and in fact was already in production for specialist commercial and military vehicles when the Phantom IV was unveiled in 1950.

The first car was commissioned for the Royal Household, and was initially planned to be unique. The Duke of Edinburgh

Park Ward offered this stunningly attractive drophead coupé body for the Silver Dawn chassis. This 1952 car was delivered to a Canadian owner when new.

The Phantom IV with its eight-cylinder engine was a very rare model, built for royalty and heads of state only. This was the first example, built for Her Majesty the Queen when she was still Princess Elizabeth. The body was by HJ Mulliner.

had tried out an experimental eight-cylinder Bentley built before the war, and had hinted strongly that an eight-cylinder engine in the new royal limousine would be very acceptable. Keen to wrest the royal warrant for cars from Daimler, Rolls-Royce pulled out all the stops to deliver what was wanted.

An order for three armoured parade cars from General Franco in Spain then persuaded the company to put the Phantom IV into limited production, but in the event only eighteen chassis were built in all, the last in 1956. Seventeen were individually bodied, one was scrapped, and deliveries were made only to heads of state and royalty, which made the Phantom IV the rarest and most exclusive Rolls-Royce of all those built since 1945.

Pictured in front of the unmistakable facade of Goodwood House, this Phantom IV has a unique landaulette body by Hooper and was built for Her Majesty the Queen in 1954.

The Best Car in the World

Whatever the weather — full ventilation, air conditioning or heating ensure a journey in complete comfort for driver and passengers of the Rolls-Royce Silver Cloud II.

The powerful 8-cylinder aluminium engine gives acceleration and performance in excess of any previous Rolls-Royce. This, together with fully automatic transmission and power-assisted steering makes it possible to maintain high average speeds without fatigue. An exceptionally high degree of safety is provided by three separate braking systems — two hydraulic and one mechanical, acting independently and in concert.

By Appointment to Her Majesty The Queen Motor Car Manufacturers Rolls-Royce Limited

CLOUDS AND PHANTOMS

THE GENERAL TREND in the motor industry towards monocoque construction in the late 1940s did not go un-noticed at Rolls-Royce's Crewe headquarters. But the company was in an almost unique position, and several factors influenced its decision to stay with separate chassis construction for the next generation of cars.

Perhaps the most important factor was that Rolls-Royce needed every component of its car designs to be as versatile as possible so that it could be used in multiple different models. This was an outcome of the rationalised range philosophy, which was still relatively new as thoughts turned to that next generation around 1950. A separate chassis could easily be produced to a common design with a variety of different wheelbase sizes; a monocoque was far harder to re-engineer for different sizes.

There was also the problem that monocoque bodies demanded very high tooling costs, which had to be amortised over the production life of a model. Rolls-Royce built cars in small numbers, and the implication was that showroom prices might have to rise in order to cover those tooling costs. This was undesirable. It was also undeniable that a proportion of customers still wanted bespoke coachwork, and that required a separate chassis, while Rolls-Royce themselves could also exploit a separate chassis by building several different body designs for it.

So a separate chassis it was. The first priority was to create a 'mainstream' model to replace the Silver Dawn and its Bentley equivalent, and from the outset the preferences of the American market were an important consideration. So the new car would have to offer more space, lighter steering, softer suspension and an automatic gearbox. It was to be called the Silver Cloud.

The magic of driving a Rolls-Royce is well encapsulated in this advertisement. The long bonnet with the famous mascot of course belongs to a Silver Cloud.

The Silver Cloud was an all-time classic design. Superbly proportioned, it looked even better with discreet two-tone colour schemes, as seen here. The car is a 1959 Silver Cloud II with V8 engine, but is visually identical to the earlier six-cylinder models.

The extra space was found by making the wheelbase 3 inches longer than in the Silver Dawn and by moving the engine forward in the chassis so that the passenger compartment could be longer. The best automatic gearboxes were those made in America, and so Rolls-Royce decided to buy in the Hydramatic type made by General Motors and to modify it to suit their requirements. Developing power assistance for the steering would take time and this would not be ready for the new model's introduction, but careful suspension design would give an appropriately compliant ride without compromising the handling. The independent front

A long-wheelbase Silver Cloud appeared in 1957, with an extra 4 inches of legroom in the rear. All the length was accommodated in the rear doors without unbalancing the profile.

suspension was also entirely redesigned as the new and much stiffer chassis took shape.

The six-cylinder engine was already being uprated for later models of the existing production cars, and there was still plenty of sales life in it. So the largest viable size of 4887cc was planned for the Silver Cloud, with a new alloy cylinder head and twin carburettors as standard. There would be no distinction in power and performance between Rolls-Royce and Bentley versions, and indeed the plan was to make the saloon versions of the two cars exactly the same – barring radiator grilles, the bonnets that fitted their differently shaped tops, and badges.

As for the body, it was designed by John Blatchley and Ivan Evernden in Crewe's own body department, and would be made by Pressed Steel again. Its design picked up on some new trends emerging around 1950, and the result was both timeless and beautifully balanced, though grander and more imposing in every way than the Silver Dawn. Although separate chassis would again be made available for those who insisted on a bespoke style, relatively few did, and this certainly contributed to the demise of at least three major bespoke coachbuilders. Freestone & Webb closed in 1958, Hooper a year later, and in 1959 Rolls-Royce bought HJ Mulliner to merge it with its Park Ward body division.

The Silver Cloud and companion Bentley S series were introduced in April 1955, and intentions caught up with

Still using the same elegant lines, Rolls-Royce created a drophead coupé through its HJ Mulliner coachbuilding division. The model was available for only four years, from 1959 to 1963. This left-hand-drive model is a Silver Cloud II version.

There were several coachbuilt designs on the Silver Cloud chassis, and this very distinctive style was by Hooper.

reality around a year later when power-assisted steering and air conditioning became available. A long-wheelbase derivative followed in 1957, with 4 extra inches in the rear compartment; standard bodies from Pressed Steel were modified appropriately by the Park Ward division. To counter the extra weight of these, the engine compression ratio was raised while both valves and carburettors were enlarged, and the more powerful engine was standardised on all models.

In the beginning, the Bentley proved more popular, probably as a legacy of the situation created by the Mk VI/R-type and Silver Dawn arrangements at the start of the decade. So overall, it was the Bentley that sold in greater numbers, although by the later 1950s the Silver Cloud had become the customer favourite and Bentley sales slowed down. Special bodies included several very attractive coupé designs for a high-performance Continental version of the Bentley chassis, and similar designs were ordered for the Silver Cloud too.

Although a late 1950s Silver Cloud was capable of a very respectable 105mph, its performance was outclassed by some rivals. A solution was in hand, though: ever since the early 1950s, Rolls-Royce had been working on a new V8 engine that would equal or better the best of those available from

American manufacturers. This was introduced in 1959 into barely modified Silver Clouds and S-series Bentleys, which became Silver Cloud II and Bentley S2 models.

The new V8 engine was heavily inspired by American practice, but it was built to meet the usual high Rolls-Royce standards of refinement. Its layout was conventional, with a single camshaft mounted in the 90-degree vee between the two banks of cylinders, but to save weight Rolls-Royce had designed the cylinder block to be cast from aluminium alloy. A design compromise had been to put the spark plugs underneath the exhaust manifolds, where access was very difficult, and some commentators felt that the engine was rougher at idle than the six-cylinder it replaced. It did add performance, though: a 6.2-litre V8-engined Silver Cloud could reach 113mph and accelerated more quickly than its predecessors through its GM-derived Hydramatic gearbox.

Power-assisted steering was now standard, and oil reservoirs needing attention just once a year had replaced the central chassis lubrication system of the first Clouds. There was, however, one notable criticism, and that was of the brakes. These were heavy cars which now had a high top speed, and the all-round drum brakes with their gearbox-driven mechanical servo were only just up to the job of stopping them. Nevertheless, the arrival of the V8 engine brought increased customer demand for the three years when the Silver Cloud II was in production. It was accompanied by the availability of

A tapering bonnet and paired headlamps brought a slightly more modern look to the Silver Cloud in 1963, and the model became the Silver Cloud III. The rest of the classic lines remained unchanged.

a two-door drophead coupé body built by HJ Mulliner and derived from the standard saloon, which went on to become a lasting favourite.

The replacement for the Silver Cloud II was, inevitably, called a Silver Cloud III (or Bentley S3), and arrived in October 1962. The engine had very slightly more power, the power steering required slightly less effort, but the brakes were still drums with a mechanical servo and the slight delay that came with it. The main changes were to the front end, modernised with four headlamps and a sloping bonnet that led to a shorter radiator grille, and to the interior, where individual front seats at last replaced the earlier split-backrest bench and a more upright rear backrest delivered more legroom.

These final separate-chassis 'mainstream' models lasted in production until late 1965. Bentleys were few and far between (although the Continental chassis proved popular and lent some of its special body styles to the Silver Cloud too). Outside of the Rolls-Royce-owned Mulliner-Park Ward body division, there were also coachbuilt bodies from James Young, but there were not many of them.

However, the Silver Cloud and its Bentley clone were not the very last separate-chassis models from Rolls-Royce. That distinction belonged to larger and far less numerous cars that bore the Phantom name and shared the essentials of their design with the Clouds. These massive cars – the largest and most expensive Rolls-Royce models ever built at the time of

The Silver Cloud dashboard, with its instruments all in the centre, was an anachronism by the time this one was fitted to a Silver Cloud III drophead coupé in 1963. The big steering wheel was looking old-fashioned, too – but the exquisite materials, fit and finish remained timeless.

For those whose budgets would not stretch to a Phantom, James Young offered their SCT100 design, the so-called 'mini-Phantom', on a Silver Cloud chassis.

their introduction – remained in production for just over thirty years, the last being built in 1990.

In line with the rationalisation scheme, the Phantom V used a longer version of the Silver Cloud chassis – extended by 22 inches and with wider axles, bigger tyres and other detail differences. It was introduced in 1959, and so always came with the then-new V8 engine. Most of those built had seven-passenger limousine bodies with a division and folding occasional seats in the rear compartment; the majority were by Mulliner-Park Ward and their lines were clearly related to those of the Silver Cloud, although there were also some by

The Phantom IV was a rare model, and this Hooper-bodied landaulette delivered to Her Majesty the Queen in May 1954 was unique among them.

This style of coachwork by Park Ward was originally introduced for the Bentley Continental chassis, and is usually known as the 'Chinese-eye' model.

Two very special Phantom V variants were built for Her Majesty the Queen. Known as the 'Canberra' vehicles, they had a roofline 5 inches higher than standard, and a glass rear dome that allowed the rear-seat occupants to be seen during a parade. This could be covered by aluminium panels when the vehicle was travelling normally.

James Young, who offered a special touring limousine design as well until they closed down for good in 1967.

The Phantom V replaced the Silver Wraith at the top of the Rolls-Royce range and was in low-volume production, to order only, for nine years. In 1962, a landaulette body became available, and the more powerful V8 engine and four-headlamp nose became standard. Just 793 chassis were built, for an average of just over 88 cars a year, and among them were two very special high-roof models built in 1960 and 1961 as state ceremonial vehicles for Her Majesty the Queen. Possibly even more famous was the one delivered to Beatle John Lennon in 1965. Originally in traditional black, it was repainted yellow in 1967 with hand-painted swirls like a gypsy caravan. The original idea for the Psychedelic

The classic formal limousine body on the Phantom V and Phantom VI chassis remained available for more than thirty years. Many were used for ceremonial duties, and this example bears a municipal coat of arms in the usual position above the windscreen.

Rolls-Royce came from fellow Beatle Ringo Starr, and the hand-painting was done by a Dutch artists' collective called The Fool.

Little changed when the Phantom V became a Phantom VI in 1968. The Silver Shadow version of the V8 engine was fitted, while separate air conditioning systems now served front and rear compartments, and there was a different facia layout. From 1972, the back doors were hung conventionally instead of rear-hinged, and from 1978 the larger 6.75-litre V8 engine arrived, together with the GM400 automatic gearbox and high-pressure braking system from the Silver Shadow.

Most Phantom VIs were built with the Mulliner-Park Ward limousine body, although there were some landaulettes and two chassis were bodied as rather ungainly convertibles by Frua in Italy. Among the 374 chassis constructed between 1968 and 1990 (an average of just over thirty-one each year) were another special high-roof state vehicle for the Queen, and a standard limousine for the same customer. All of them were splendid – but hugely admired – anachronisms by the time the last one was built.

Two Phantom VI chassis were shipped to Italy and were bodied as convertibles by the coachbuilder Frua in Moncalieri near Turin. Each car was different. This is the earlier one, completed in 1973 for a Swiss diplomat. It is to Frua's credit that he made such a good job of the lines of this gigantic two-door body.

SHADOWS, SPIRITS
AND SERAPHS

THE LAST THIRD of the twentieth century brought new challenges for the Rolls-Royce car division. Serious new rivals appeared on the scene – not least the Mercedes-Benz 600 of 1963 and the same company's S-class saloons from 1972 – while rapidly changing new technology robbed the company of its ability to remain ahead of the game all the time. Manufacturing costs also escalated, and these could only be amortised by long model runs and by sub-models that shared their fundamental engineering with the mainstream cars.

In addition, excessive costs in the Rolls-Royce aero engine division nearly ran the whole show off the rails in 1971 when the Rolls-Royce Group went bankrupt. Fortunately, cars and aero engines were separated; the company was first subsidised and then nationalised, and the car division thrived

The Silver Shadow was a more square-rigged design than the Silver Cloud it replaced, but was very much in tune with its times. This is a 1974 'flared-arch' model; the car once belonged to rock singer Freddie Mercury.

as Rolls-Royce Motors under new ownership by engineering giant Vickers after 1980.

The major challenge came early on, as Rolls-Royce finally embraced a monocoque structure for its new Silver Shadow model. The car was a huge step forward: it was also the first Rolls-Royce with all-independent suspension and with disc brakes, and it used advanced high-pressure hydraulic systems for both of these new features. To minimise noise transmission, the two sub-frames that carried the running gear were insulated from the body by rubber bushes, but that same concern deterred the company from switching to modern radial tyres, at least initially.

Its shape was carefully conservative, rather slab-sided by comparison with the curvaceous Silver Cloud range but very much in tune with the trends of the mid-1960s. The wood-and-leather interior was as luxurious as ever, and 120mph performance was available from the 6.25-litre V8 engine, re-engineered from its Silver Cloud form and now with accessibly relocated spark plugs. Automatic was standard, the left-hand-drive cars having a new American-made three-speed gearbox although the right-hand-drive models retained the

The long-wheelbase variant of the Silver Shadow was known as the Silver Wraith II from 1977. This 1978 example shows the heavy black bumpers developed for the US market and standard across the range from 1977.

The two-door Silver Shadow was built by the Mulliner-Park Ward division from 1966, and this example was the company demonstrator, looking superb in Rolls-Royce Regal Red paint.

older four-speed until 1968. As was to be expected, there were near-identical Bentley versions as well (called T-series models), and from 1969 a long-wheelbase model with 4 extra inches in the wheelbase and the option of a division was introduced.

The major changes over the fifteen years of Silver Shadow production were driven by customer demand for better handling dynamics and the tightening safety and exhaust emissions requirements of the US market. Radial tyres finally arrived in 1972, accompanied by a new 'compliant suspension' that damped out road noise, and then wider tracks in 1974 were accompanied by discreetly flared wheel arches. To simplify manufacture, all Silver Shadows had the US Federal specification after May 1969, with safety-related interior changes and engine modifications to reduce exhaust emissions. When these modifications threatened to reduce power output unacceptably, Rolls-Royce engineers developed a 6.75-litre version of the V8 engine and made it standard from summer 1970. Further-developed versions of that same engine remained in production (latterly for Bentley models) until well into the twenty-first century.

American regulations also demanded impact-absorbing bumpers, and from 1977 the Silver Shadow II carried large black bumpers to suit. At the same time, the long-wheelbase model was renamed Silver Wraith II. These final models also had further revised suspension and – for California only, where emissions controls were tighter – fuel injection instead of carburettors.

Moving to monocoque construction sounded the death-knell for the traditional coachbuilt Rolls-Royce. New bodies had to be engineered, as well as designed, so that they would cope with the stresses that a monocoque was designed to withstand, and the coachbuilders who had traditionally worked with Rolls-Royce and Bentley products were simply not equipped to deal with that. Although James Young built 50 two-door conversions of the standard four-door body in 1967, they had little to commend them except exclusivity, and Young's went under soon afterwards.

Rolls-Royce, meanwhile, was determined to offer an alternative to the standard saloon that had the appeal of a traditional coachbuilt model. The solution it developed was what might be called a 'standard coachbuilt' car – a supremely elegant two-door design that would be hand finished by its Mulliner-Park Ward division.

The two-door Shadow appeared as a saloon ('coupé' in the USA) in 1966 and as a convertible in 1967. Both types were

With an enlarged engine, the two-door models were renamed Corniche in 1970. This is the Corniche convertible, a model that would go on to have a very long production life.

characterised by a gentle kick-up in the lines just ahead of the rear wheels, giving the body much more character than the nearly straight lines of the standard car. The first cars shared their mechanical specification with the standard saloons, but from early 1971 Rolls-Royce gave the two-door cars a clearer identity of their own. They were renamed Corniche models, gained a more powerful version of the latest 6.75-litre engine, and were visually distinguished by different wheel trims and a new dashboard.

The Corniche had exactly the customer appeal that Rolls-Royce had intended. The closed versions remained in production (with both Rolls-Royce and Bentley badges) until 1981, but the convertibles lasted another thirteen years, finally going out of production in 1994 after a twenty-seven-year run. After 1979, they had been progressively updated with mechanical and other elements from the contemporary Silver Spirit saloons, and the last Rolls-Royce variants were known as Corniche IV types; the Bentley had meanwhile been re-named a Continental in 1984.

Yet even the Corniche was not enough to satisfy all the potential customers for a top-model Rolls-Royce, and so in 1975 the company introduced yet another special body

The Camargue shared its underpinnings with the Corniche, but its Italian styling was always controversial. This was the Rolls-Royce flagship model of the time.

on the Silver Shadow platform. The new car was called the Camargue, and its two-door body had been designed by leading Italian coachbuilder Pininfarina, although it was built in Britain. Originally intended to replace the Corniche, it became an additional model after a product review prompted by the 1971 break from Rolls-Royce Ltd.

The Camargue's appearance was always controversial, and a major element of its appeal was really its exclusivity. It did have a world-first automatic split-level climate control system, but many onlookers thought it looked like a big Fiat. With few mechanical differences from the Corniche, it nevertheless sold to the very wealthy customers Rolls-Royce had in mind and, like the Corniche, it outlived its Silver Shadow parent by several years. Just 530 were built between 1975 and 1986, a total of just under 50 a year. Though hardly

Although the Silver Spirit looked very different from the Silver Shadow, underneath it was a further-developed version of that car. This is an early example.

For those who wanted a coachbuilt derivative of the Spirit, Hooper produced a number of these two-door models that were converted from the standard bodyshell. Some cars were made even more distinctive with wire wheels.

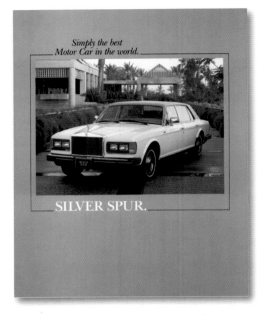

Simply the best Motor Car in the world.

SILVER SPUR.

American regulations demanded separate headlamps for main and dipped beams, and the light units had to conform to certain standards. This is a US-model Silver Spur, the long-wheelbase version of the Silver Spirit.

pretty, the Camargue certainly did have presence – and that was what mattered to those who bought one.

The huge cost of getting the Shadow into production ensured that much of its engineering would be carried over to the next generation of Rolls-Royce models, and so when the new Silver Spirit arrived in 1980 it brought an all-new body on what were really further evolved Shadow underpinnings. The body design was another in-house creation, and this time costs meant there would be no alternative 'semi-coachbuilt' derivatives: Rolls-Royce kept the Corniche and Camargue in production instead. From the start, the major effort went into improving ride quality, and a long-wheelbase model arrived a year into production. Known by the separate name of Silver Spur, this was now built with the usual extra 4 inches of wheelbase length rather than converted from a standard body.

Nevertheless, the Silver Spirit certainly did sire multiple offspring. Its evolutionary mechanical improvements were reflected on contemporary Corniche and Camargue models, too. There were Bentley derivatives, called Mulsanne, and from 1982 the high-performance Bentley Turbo initiated a new line of development that would give the Bentley marque a new and separate existence.

Quite clearly, the Rolls-Royce name still attracted wealthy buyers: in 1983, the Rolls-Royce dealer in Beverly Hills, California, sold 65 cars – and 61 customers paid in cash. Demand led to the creation of ultra-long-wheelbase derivatives, designed and initially built for Rolls-Royce by Robert Jankel, a custom building specialist. Two six-door Jankel limousines built for the Sultan of Brunei were the longest Rolls-Royce cars ever made when new in the early 1980s. One was for the Sultan, the other for his latest wife. The revived coachbuilder Hooper also built a number of two-door conversions from the late 1980s; one, for a Middle Eastern princess, had 24-carat gold-plated brightwork, including on the exhaust pipe.

Meanwhile, the Silver Spirit itself gradually evolved into Mk II (1989), Mk III (1993) and Mk IV (1995) models, although the latter was more usually known as the New Silver Spirit. There was a special Flying Spur turbocharged edition, too, in 1994. Production theoretically ended in 1997, but in practice Spirits were built into 1999, partly to help offset resistance to the new Silver Seraph in the USA.

The Silver Seraph arrived as the replacement for the Silver Spirit in 1998 – a most inconvenient time for Rolls-Royce because that was the year ownership of the company changed. The Seraph's design had been compromised to a degree by limited resources: in the early 1990s, Rolls-Royce had recognised that they needed to modernise their manufacturing plant in order to keep ahead of the game, and the costs of building a new factory at Crewe impacted heavily on the development budget for the Seraph.

The V8 engine first seen in 1959 powered all the Shadow and Spirit models, and their derivatives. This is a 6.75-litre version, pictured in a 1972 Silver Shadow.

The main casualty was that the company could not afford to design the new engine it needed to replace the long-serving V8. So, after evaluating several options, they concluded a deal with BMW in Germany for the supply of that company's 5.4-litre V12 for the Silver Seraph, and for a twin-turbocharged V8 to

There were several ultra-long wheelbase models based on the Silver Spirit. This is the Silver Spur Park Ward, dating from around 1998.

Longer still is this Touring Limousine, again by Park Ward. Note the longer side windows, which give a better balance to the design than the short intermediate window on the Silver Spur Park Ward.

power its Bentley Arnage equivalent. BMW would also supply some of the switchgear and the air conditioning system for the new car. Several engineering consultancies helped out on the design, too: Lotus, for example, designed the suspension, while Mayflower did the body engineering. At least Rolls-Royce was able to construct the entire bodyshell itself for the first time, in the new plant at Crewe.

The Seraph was designed to look smaller than it really was, partly to counter growing environmental concerns about pollution from large cars. Some criticised it as bland. There

The Silver Seraph was a more rounded design, and its designer, Graham Hull, took inspiration from the Silver Cloud of the 1950s. This is a US-market example, dating from 1999 and pictured at a marque enthusiasts' gathering.

was only a standard-wheelbase car at launch in March 1998, and a long-wheelbase model (called the Park Ward after the in-house coachbuilder) did not arrive until early 2001 with an extra 10 inches of length.

The new V12 engine, an exemplary piece of engineering, delivered 140mph performance, but the Silver Seraph was deliberately designed as a car to cosset its owners. Buyers who wanted blistering acceleration were gently steered towards the Bentley Arnage. Engine and differential had been mounted directly to the body shell so that the sub-frame mountings could be tuned for optimum comfort, and a sophisticated active ride control system was standard.

Yet the Silver Seraph was never really able to fulfil its promise, and customer concerns over the protracted sale of Rolls-Royce in 1998 must have hurt sales. Just 1,570 cars were built in four years – an average of less than 400 a year – before the Seraph was taken out of production in 2002. Its Bentley equivalent, by contrast, remained in production under new ownership until 2009.

The name on the acoustic engine cover reads 'Silver Seraph', but underneath is a BMW 5.4-litre V12 engine, bought in because Rolls-Royce could not afford to design their own new engine in the mid-1990s.

Wood, leather and a general aura of well-being: this was the dashboard of a Silver Seraph, which followed in the great Rolls-Royce tradition.

GERMAN OWNERSHIP

ENGINEERING GROUP VICKERS decided to sell off its automotive interests in 1998 to focus on its core business, and Rolls-Royce was put on the market. BMW's close relationship with the company, as a supplier of engines and other components for both Rolls-Royce and Bentley cars, immediately made it a front runner among likely new owners. However, at the last minute the Volkswagen Group trumped BMW's purchase offer of £340 million by one of £430 million.

That Bentley would now belong to the Volkswagen Group was never really in dispute, but BMW were determined to fight hard over the Rolls-Royce brand. A complicated and messy series of moves and counter-moves, negotiations and veiled threats then followed. Eventually, the deadlock was broken in July 1998. Broadly speaking, from 1 January 2003, full rights to manufacture Rolls-Royce cars would belong to BMW, and full rights to manufacture Bentley cars would belong to Volkswagen. But Volkswagen would retain all the old Rolls-Royce assets, including the Crewe factory. All BMW really gained was the right to use the name, the grille shape and the Spirit of Ecstasy mascot on motor cars.

As an interim arrangement, the existing Bentley and Rolls-Royce models would continue to be built at the VW-owned factory in Crewe. BMW agreed to continue supplying engines for the cars and would allow use of the Rolls-Royce name on cars built at Crewe. So the pressure was on BMW to develop a new Rolls-Royce and build the factory to assemble it within the remarkably short period of three and a half years. It is to their credit that they achieved both targets, the new factory being erected at Goodwood in Sussex and the new Rolls-Royce Phantom reaching the showrooms during 2003.

The dashboard design of the Phantom Series II was remarkably uncluttered, despite the wealth of on-board technology. Interestingly, the traditional wood trim is absent from this Phantom Series II Drophead Coupé.

Bridging the gap between the old and the new was the Corniche V, a classic convertible model with a well-established name, which combined mechanical underpinnings developed for a Bentley with styling cues from the Silver Seraph.

The new makers of Rolls-Royce motor cars were now known as Rolls-Royce Motor Cars Ltd.

One splendid anachronism bridged the gap during this uncertain period. There had been no convertible Rolls-Royce since 1994, when the last Corniche IV had been built, and the marque's custodians believed there would be custom for a new one. In order to minimise costs, they based it on the existing Bentley Azure convertible, which was powered by the latest development of the long-serving 6.75-litre V8 engine. Body styling cues were taken from the Silver Seraph, and the new car became the Rolls-Royce Corniche V. It was a rare example of a new Rolls-Royce being based on an existing Bentley rather than the other way round.

The new Corniche was introduced in early 2000 and was built at Crewe for just under two years, the last example leaving

The new Phantom was a massive car in all its forms. This is in fact an Extended Wheelbase model dating from 2012, with the longer rear doors characteristic of the model.

The Phantom Drophead Coupé sat on a shorter wheelbase than the saloon, and of course had only two doors. The tail lights and styling lines on the flanks were those of the parent car. By the end of production, Rolls-Royce were calling it a Phantom VII.

the assembly lines in August 2002. Symbolically perhaps, it was also the very last Rolls-Royce car to be built at Crewe before the plant was turned over entirely to Bentley assembly. Just 384 of these 135mph Corniche V models had been built.

The new Phantom for 2003 was the seventh Rolls-Royce model to bear that name, but carried no number to indicate this. It was nevertheless conceived as a low-volume, ultra-expensive grand limousine in the tradition of earlier Phantoms, and would be built only to individual order. BMW planned to use it as their technology flagship, and designed for it a special 6.75-litre V12 engine after rejecting a planned 9-litre V16 as too extravagant.

The original Phantom front end design with its slit-like headlights and round driving lamps is seen here on a bespoke Phantom Drophead Coupé dating from 2011.

The Phantom models became Series II types for 2012, but retained the essential lines of the original. Even careful design was unable to disguise the sheer size of the car.

The Phantom's body was constructed from lightweight aluminium, and the car ran on air suspension to give top-quality ride comfort. The body design was undeniably imposing, but some commentators found it hard to relate to the Rolls-Royce cars that had gone before. Slit-like headlamps gave it a very distinctive appearance, while rear-hinged 'coach doors' eased entry and exit from the rear seats, and of course there was a massive list of options available through the Rolls-Royce Bespoke programme. As in the marque's 1930s heyday, customers could ask for anything within reason to personalise their cars.

The Phantom range was developed through an Extended Wheelbase model in 2005, which added nearly 10 inches of rear legroom. In 2007 came a two-door Drophead Coupé

There was increasing demand for two-tone paint schemes, which worked well on these large cars. This 2012 Phantom drophead coupé shows the redesigned front end of the Series II cars.

The Ghost was introduced in 2010 as the smaller Rolls-Royce model – but it was still a big car. This one, finished in Rose Quartz with a Gunmetal metallic bonnet, was a special order for Dubai. Demand for bespoke models such as this one accounted for 56 per cent of Ghost sales in 2011.

The Extended Wheelbase version of the Ghost offered as much lounging room as most rear-seat passengers could wish for. Note the provision of three seat belts so that a third passenger could be legally carried if the need arose.

derivative on a wheelbase shortened by 10 inches, and this was followed a year later by a Phantom coupé of the same size. Sales increased year on year, boosted by small-volume limited editions, some tailored specifically for certain markets such as China, where Rolls-Royce had been able to exploit the booming economy to advantage. That same year saw the availability of an armoured version of the full-size Phantom as well.

The Phantom was facelifted in 2012 and sales remained strong, aided as before by special editions. Production of all derivatives was brought to an end in early 2016, by which time the full-size car had been on sale for thirteen years, and Rolls-Royce promised a new Phantom in 2018.

The Phantom and its offshoots were never intended to be the only models from BMW's Rolls-Royce company. However, it would be seven years before the anticipated smaller Rolls-Royce entered production, this one more of a direct replacement for the long-defunct Silver Seraph. The Rolls-Royce Ghost, introduced in 2010, was still a large car, though, and its wheelbase of 129.7 inches was just an inch shorter that than of the two-door Phantoms and 7 inches longer than that of a Silver Seraph.

The new 'small' Rolls-Royce shared around 20 per cent of its

The Ghost was recognisably from the same family as the larger Phantom. This hugely attractive two-tone model dates from 2012.

parts with the latest BMW 7 Series saloons, although the common features were not visible. Unlike the Phantom, the Ghost was constructed of steel. Its engine was also unique, a 6.6-litre twin-turbo V12 that boasted 570PS and made this car the most powerful Rolls-Royce ever built. It was very quick, too, not least so that it could counter rival saloons from Volkswagen-owned Bentley; Rolls-Royce claimed a 0–60mph sprint time of 4.7 seconds – and that for a car weighing nearly 5500lb (2495kg).

Ever since the Silver Clouds of the 1950s, the standard four-door saloon had been accompanied sooner or later by a long-wheelbase derivative, and the Ghost Extended Wheelbase model arrived in 2011 with an extra 6.7 inches

The Wraith two-door coupé with its stylish sloping rear achieved the difficult trick of retaining an impressive presence and combining that with a distinctly sporting appearance.

(170mm) between wheel centres. A limited-edition V-Spec model with 600PS was available on the standard wheelbase in the first half of 2014, just before the facelifted Series II Ghost was introduced, with new LED headlights and some interior changes.

Again following familiar Rolls-Royce practice, the Ghost was developed to provide two-door

'personal' derivatives. The first to appear was the Rolls-Royce Wraith, a four-seat coupé on a shortened wheelbase of 122.5 inches that reached showrooms in 2013. It was followed in 2015 by the Rolls-Royce Dawn, a convertible on the same wheelbase and with visual similarities but with what the company claimed were 80 per cent different panels.

All these new models sold extremely well. Sales of the Phantom in 2003 had been just 300 cars, but by 2014 Rolls-Royce sales for all models combined had risen to 4,063 cars for the calendar year. Like other luxury car makers, the company had been able to exploit the huge growth in new markets such as China and Russia, and regular special editions continued to keep interest alive from buyers who wanted a car that was just a little bit different from that which their friends or colleagues had. It was not coachbuilding in the way that had been understood in the 1930s, but it was appealing very successfully to the modern descendants of those who had been Rolls-Royce customers eighty years earlier.

So, more than 110 years after the first Rolls-Royce motor car had made exceptional standards of quality available to those who could afford to pay for it, the marque still stood for the same values. It was becoming slowly more successful, too, and in 2015 announced plans for a completely new departure – a Rolls-Royce SUV that would be introduced in 2017 and which would compete with the Bentley Bentayga SUV that arrived in 2016. It looked as if the legendary marque was in safe hands.

There was necessarily less room in the passenger cabin of the Wraith, but there was certainly no shortage of the traditional luxury features.

The great traditions remained alive and well under BMW ownership. This was the tread-plate on the door sill of a Rolls-Royce Ghost.

FURTHER READING

There is no shortage of books about the Rolls-Royce marque. For anyone who is interested in finding out more about the cars that figure in this book, the following books are a selection with which to start.

Bobbitt, Malcolm. Rolls-Royce Silver Spirit & Silver Spur; Bentley Mulsanne, etc. Veloce Publishing, 2000.

Gentile, Raymond. *The Rolls-Royce Phantom II Continental*. Dalton Watson Ltd, 1980.

Taylor, James. *Original Rolls-Royce and Bentley 1946–1965*. Herridge & Sons, 2008 (earlier edition 1999 by Bay View Books).

Walker, Nick. *Rolls-Royce 20hp, 20/25, 25/30 & Wraith, In Detail*. Herridge & Sons, 2009.

PLACES TO VISIT

Atwell-Wilson Motor Museum, Stockley Lane, Calne,
  Wiltshire SN11 0NF. Telephone: 01249 813119.
  Website: www.atwellwilson.org.uk
Beaulieu National Motoring Museum, Beaulieu, New Forest,
  Hampshire SO42 7ZN. Telephone: 01590 612345.
  Website: www.beaulieu.co.uk
British Motor Museum, Banbury Road, Gaydon,
  Warwickshire, CV35 0BJ. Telephone: 01926 641188.
  Website: www.britishmotormuseum.co.uk
Caister Castle Motor Museum, Caister Castle, Castle Lane,
  Caister-on-Sea, Great Yarmouth, Norfolk, NR30 5SN.
  Telephone: 01664 567707. Website: www.caistercastle.co.uk
Cotswold Motoring Museum & Toy Collection, The Old Mill,
  Bourton-on-the-Water, Gloucestershire GL54 2BY.
  Telephone: 01451 821255.
  Website: www.cotswoldmotoringmuseum.co.uk
Coventry Transport Museum, Millennium Place, Hales Street,
  Coventry CV1 1JD. Telephone: 024 7623 4270.
  Website: www.transport-museum.com
Haynes International Motor Museum, Sparkford, Yeovil,
  Somerset BA22 7LH. Telephone: 01963 440804.
  Website: www.haynesmotormuseum.com
London Motor Museum, 3 Nestles Avenue, Hayes, UB3 4SB.
  Telephone: 0800 195 0777.
  Website: www.londonmotormuseum.co.uk
Moretonhampstead Motor Museum, The Old Bus Depot,
  Court St, Moretonhampstead, Devon TQ13 8LG.
  Telephone: 01647 440636.
  Website: moretonmotormuseum.co.uk

INDEX